'How to hypnotise anyone!'

Confessions of a Rogue Hypnotist.

By the Rogue Hypnotist

Disclaimer: the Rogue Hypnotist accepts no legal liability for the use or misuse of the information contained in this book. People who are not qualified professionals use the information at their own risk. This book is intended for entertainment and educational purposes only. Only the hypnosis scripts, deepeners contained within are for your personal or public use copyright free. They may not be resold.

CONTENTS

ACKNOWLEDGMENTS

To all the people who made this book an international number 1 bestseller on Amazon! I want to have your children!

Introduction: why read my book on hypnosis?

Good question? Mainly because unlike all the other ones out there – the skills I will teach you will work pretty much 100% of the time.

My hope is that this book will be of use to stage hypnotists, hypnotherapist, NLPers, the beginner, the student of psychology, the amateur enthusiast and even the merely curious! By the way you don't have to agree with everything I say; often I'm saying it to stimulate thought on your part. Some of the things I say will be generalisations: so there's always the exception!

This book and the information within is not a replacement for proper training in hypnosis or hypnotherapy. To be a full professional you need the right training.

After reading this book I hope you'll begin to see how hypnosis is going on all around you quite a lot of the time! I'll give examples from advertising and 'the media' too.

All of the hypnotic skills and modules in which I teach you will interrelate: I want you to have my expertise and skill honed down and ready for use. It should take you weeks to do what took me years to learn.

I'll teach you how to do 'embedded commands' properly, how to make up your own hypnotic language, where to focus people's attention, how to get genuine 'rapport': the lot! I'll dispel the myths and let you know the truth. How do I know this? Because I've tried it all: I know what works and what doesn't from real life success. Trial and error. I made the errors so you won't have to. This book will save you time and energy! All you need to know is here: I've crystallised it, separated wheat from chaff!

This is a 'how to' book: any theory will help your practical skills. My intent is that you'll be able to create your own hypnotic inductions using the principles herein. If you want to be good at anything you need to learn the principles, the rest is easy.

I am a professional hypnotist. I am qualified: I am an Advanced Master Practitioner of NLP; I am a professional hypnotherapist and psychotherapist. I am an expert in treating pain using hypnosis. I am an expert in treating anxiety disorders and all manner of addictions. I know what I am doing. I have all the certificates; I've read all the books, gone to all the classes, I was taught by all the best people.

The other reason you should read this is because I am a very good hypnotist: I have an incredibly high success rate in my private practise in London England helping people.

I have written this book in a (I hope) a fun, amusing, memorable and readable style rather than all the dry, pseudo-academic books on hypnotherapy written by psychologists who clearly can't hypnotise a zombie!

And now I want to teach you how to hypnotise anyone. Relax – it's easy – everyone can be hypnotised.

Before we proceed, a warning – *never use your knowledge of hypnosis to harm anyone, or impose your ideas, wishes, wants and desires on others. If you do - expect to pay a price! Why would you want to manipulate someone anyway? That's what psychopaths do. Use your new knowledge to help others and to protect you and those you love from 'undue influence.'*

You are fully responsible for what you do with this knowledge I am about to teach you. The only reason I learnt about hypnosis was to help others. That's why my client's trust me: I am genuine and I care. By the end of this first book in my 'Confessions of a Rogue Hypnotist,' series you will be able to hypnotise anyone just using words. That is my promise to you.

The mystery of hypnosis?

Ok I had to get the last paragraph out of the way. I am assuming people who read this are ethical. Although I don't want to be too hypocritical – I once stole a book on ethics. Now that bit is out of the way – shall we begin?

Everyone can be hypnotised. You have been hypnotised at some time in your life. You may even be hypnotised now for all I know!

There are obviously exceptions to these sweeping though truthful statements. Brain damaged people, exceptionally stupid people and highly scared people may prove trickier to hypnotise but maybe not – given enough time. Women and children are much easier to hypnotise than men. Although it's easy to hypnotise men too.

Hypnosis is a natural state. It is not the same as trance. Hypnosis, which is a daft term really but we're stuck with it, is just a highly focused state – *hypnosis is a state of intense absorption or concentration* - that is it. Everyone has experienced this state. You can do it with your eyes wide open. If you are doing something that fully absorbs your attention so that you ignore distractions then you have experienced hypnosis. And everyone has. The man who coined the term hypnosis regretted it latter and tried to call it 'Monoideism'; that is focusing on one thing. Unsurprisingly that nugget of a term never caught on.

So what is trance? Trance is just the daydream state – everyone daydreams. You daydream. You have to. It's a way to go inside and solve problems, access your imagination and creativity, a way to take a break from outside stimuli for a while. It is essential to good mental health as long as it is purposeful. I say this because depression or what we call depression is a trance state too, just not a very pleasant one!

Hypnotic trance (that is the combination of both previously mentioned states) is the unique state a hypnotherapist and stage hypnotist may utilise (if they know how) to help people heal themselves or to entertain people. Though personally I find stage hypnosis shows very boring and dull affairs.

Nobody really knows what hypnosis is and how or why it works. If they tell you they do, they don't - they are just guessing, speculating – nobody knows – it remains a mystery. Its neural mechanics remain a mystery. It is of course possible that some underground advanced scientific lab exists somewhere where all hypnosis secrets are known but if it does exist those boffins aren't sharing. So you don't need to know how it works - just that it does. However the mechanics or art of hypnotising anyone is very easy to learn. Anyone can hypnotise someone else and anyone can be hypnotised. In fact you've done both already.

Most hypnotists, hypnotherapists do not induce hypnosis in their clients, they induce relaxation. I will talk more about this later on. Relaxation is not essential to get a hypnotic state. Terrified people are highly hypnotisable. A patient awaiting surgery is in a profound hypnotic state. That is why it is essential that surgeons and nurses in operating rooms are careful what they say. A patient undergoing surgery can hear _everything_ that is being said in an operating room – at an unconscious level.

In such a state the unconscious mind or subconscious mind (you could call it Fred if you want!) takes things very literally. It would be interesting to know how many surgeons had inadvertently caused a patient to die from a heart attack during on operation by saying the wrong thing. Comatose people can hear everything that is said in their environment; just because their conscious mind is offline don't assume they can't hear – _you can't switch your ears off_. When you sleep your ears are not closed. This is probably why Aldous Huxley wrote about sleep programming (hypnopaedia) in his horrific Brave New World. If you give suggestions to a sleeping person they may well act upon them.

You don't need to speak in a quiet and relaxing voice to get hypnosis – you can bark orders like a Sargent Major. Swat teams will burst into buildings pointing guns at people and scream 'Get on the *&$ing floor! Arms in the air!' etc. You had better believe those other people in the room they are threatening go instantly into a hypnoidal state.

However we aren't going to use hypnosis to be ordering others around. We are using it to help in a way that feels very good. I'll start to show you how it's done as you read on. I've started already actually!

The fundamentals for inducing hypnotic trance.

The best way to help someone achieve a state of hypnotic trance is to get them to focus their attention inside. Now what do I mean by 'inside'? I mean focus their attention on bodily sensations, feelings, pleasant fantasies, pleasant daydreams, pleasant memories (do not access traumatic memories!), imaginative scenes, pleasant sounds – this can be music, a kind voice, the sound of a babbling brook. Even the evocation of delightful smells (powerfully associative and note: women's sense of smell is greater than men's) will work wonders. Effectively you direct attention to the 'internal senses' as opposed to the external. In hypnosis the external environment is ignored for a while and to varying degrees according to the 'depth' of hypnosis.

Hypnotic skill 1: Narrowing the focus of attention.

If you start an induction by getting someone to focus on their breathing, doing nothing to it but noticing it they will start to enter hypnosis – why? *Because you are beginning to focus their attention on one thing to the exclusion of everything else.* This is why some hypnotists ask someone to stare at a spot, a candle flame. This is why the TV is exceptionally hypnotic. If a person is watching a programme that absorbs them totally they will be wholly unaware of the people around them, the feeling of the shoes on their feet, sounds in the street. They are in a deep hypnotic trance: an eyes open trance. Because they don't know they are – they are suggestible – their analytical guard is down. Who knew the TV induced hypnotic trance? I didn't, till I leaned about hypnosis.

Soap operas grab the attention of women – they are concerned with the drama of relationships and emotions. Men can be hypnotised easily through pornography (sexual fantasy) and through sports which is vicarious tribal warfare. Men can also have their attention 'locked' by telling them that their family/tribe is in danger. Men and boys naturally scan the environment for potential danger at an unconscious level. This is due to their wild genetic heritage of protecting the women and children of the tribe. As Aristotle pointed out in his 'Rhetoric' – this fact has been exploited through political propaganda for millennia.

Women tend to make up the majority of any hypnotherapist's clients. Why? Women are more likely than men to try new things: this is well known. Women's magazines also focus women's minds on health and beauty concerns – including so called 'alternative therapies.' Women are more likely than men to take action to solve health problems. Being more emotional and intuitive than men they are more open to the idea that something like hypnosis could work. Hypnosis uses words – women are highly susceptible to emotional manipulation through language because they process words through both 'hemispheres' of the brain. Thus _all_ words have a potentially emotive effect on women. If you can evoke an emotion in someone you are accessing unconscious processes and so you are well on your way to hypnotising them. Simply asking someone,

'How do you **feel** about x?'

will elicit an unconscious response that bypasses critical thinking. TV reporters frequently ask this kind of question. If you wanted a conscious response you would ask,

*'What do you **think** about x?'*

By the way asking a question is hypnotic, any question requires that someone 'go inside' and retrieve the information asked for. Depending on the type of question asked the 'hypnotic response' will be greater or lesser.

Hypnotic script 1: A narrowing focus induction.

This is my variation of what is known in the trade as the 'Betty Erickson Induction.' It was used by the wife of the great hypnotherapist Dr. Milton Erickson. Use a slower, more relaxing voice than normal and read out loud. The pause indicated by ... should last between 3-5 seconds. You need to give subjects time to process what you say. Words that are highlighted are embedded commands – such as you can **calm down**. When saying them pause just before you say the command and use a downward inflexion as you would when making a 'command statement' not a rising one used for questions. Best to try these things with willing friends or relatives at first if you've never done this sort of thing before.

Betty Erickson Induction.

'Notice four things you can see in the room...
four objects...
maybe the way the light hits an object...
Now notice three things you can see...
Now two...
Now one...
That's right...
Just gently...
close your eyes...

Notice four sounds in the environment...
maybe that airplane, the ticking clock...
a certain quality of my voice if you prefer...
Now three sounds...
Now two...
Now one...
Now notice four feelings or sensations...
could be the feel of your palm touching your
jeans perhaps...
the sofa beneath you...
the feel of the shirt on your neck...
Good.
Now three things you feel...
Now two...
Now one...
That's right.
(You can continue with this if you want...though
the above is enough however the following can
serve as a little deepener...)
*Now, can you **imagine** four pleasant objects*
that you've seen...?
could be a cat...
a dog...
a cup...anything...
And when you've done that
imagine three things you've seen...
And two when you're ready...
And one.
Ok...Very good...
now recall four pleasant sounds with your
mind's ear...

a steam train chugging by...
children laughing
a piano playing...
anything you like...
When you've done that
recall more sounds...
Two sounds...
And then just one...
one sound only...
Good, now
can you remember four pleasant sensations?
four textures...
Maybe a cat's fur...
the taste of ice cream...
the feel of the breeze against your skin...
whatever you'd like to imagine feeling...
that's right...
Now, when you're ready...
three things you've felt...
And then two when you're ready...
And one...
That's right.
Perfect.
You're doing fantastically.
(Note how I am also *counting down* which is
suggestive of deepening trance. Now you must
wake them up – called 'exduction.' Perform this
part with a gradually more energised and
rousing voice.)
I am now going to count from 1-3
and on 3 you'll be fully wide awake,

*back to full waking consciousness feeling
fantastic!
Ok and 1, more aware of your body
and the room around you!
2, all unnecessary relaxation leaving the body...
feeling wide awake and totally reenergised!
And you can open eyes feeling great! On 3!'*

Being careful where you send the brain.

A good hypnotist must *use language precisely and with caution*. Be careful where and when you send a person's brain. If for example you have a person suffering from 'anxiety' do not ask them to vividly remember the last time they were really anxious – that is just stupid. Rather ask them to remember the last time they felt relaxed. *Hypnosis is an amplifying state* – whatever you draw attention to in its induction or maintenance will be intensified. When inducing hypnosis you can direct a person's attention to where they already feel most calm in the body.

A note and warning: *it is **never** necessary to dig into past events, pain and trauma in order to help someone. In fact doing so is potentially deeply dangerous; in a vulnerable person it is possible it could trigger a psychotic break.*

To be safe you can say something like,

'Only pleasant thoughts, pleasant images drift through your mind...'

You are taking someone on a journey. Make it nice. If someone does 'abreact,' which I have never had happen simply say...

'That image can turn to black and white and fade off into the distance until it vanishes completely as you open your eyes, feeling calm and aware of your surroundings fully.'

What is the subconscious/unconscious?

Good question! There are various models of the brain/nervous system and how it operates. Instead of calling the part a hypnotist speaks to 'the subconscious' or 'unconscious' it is better to refer to what I call *'other than conscious processes.'*

Think about it this way: people will often refer to the 'back of the mind' as being the subconscious and the foreground of the mind as the conscious. This may be because our senses are located at the front of our head, who knows - however the 'subconscious' is really just the part of the mind-body system that controls and runs everything outside of conscious awareness.

A part of your mind is digesting the last meal you ate and utilising it for your body's actual needs. Technically this part is known as the enteric nervous system: it is very much a second brain and almost semi-autonomous from the brain in your head. It is the origin of the terms 'gut instincts,' 'gut reaction', 'I felt it in my guts.' This is the 'part' you work with when treating IBS (Irritable Bowel Syndrome,) stress related constipation and diarrhoea or stomach pain.

Another part of you is regulating blood flow 24 hours a day: blood flow can be influenced in hypnosis to cure warts, heal wounds and stop bleeding during surgery. Some part of you breathes for you without your having to think about it. Bet you just noticed your breathing. This is why it is hypnotic for the hypnotist to ask a person to notice their breathing and then to change the rate of breathing – effectively they are altering an unconscious process which is itself hypnotic.

Think about it: instinctively a woman's body knows how to grow a healthy baby. It needs no conscious help at all – it just does it.

It seems the deepest parts of the human psyche's main aim is to keep you alive and well: *when this instinct is thwarted or threatened people can develop 'psychological health problems.'*

By the way the medical model of disease is antithetical to the hypnotic one: in hypnotherapy mental health problems are seen as sane yet ultimately unhelpful responses to real stressors. Anxiety is not a 'disease' it is the mind-body system's normal response to a person's natural needs not being met; much as pain is a natural response to injury. Pain is also a signal that the subconscious can and will use if a person should fail to make the right changes in their life not just as a warning to prevent further injury. Such problems should really be seen as a response much like a thermostat's - trying to maintain a regular level of heat. By the way your subconscious does that on your behalf to. It makes you sweat.

To conclude, the mind-body system is one interconnected unit – they are not separate but both intimately affect the other – this has been known for a long time. Using hypnosis you can *significantly* affect the mind-body system – people can become hypnotically blind and deaf (Erickson did this in the early 20th century,) allergic reactions can be stopped in their tracks and reversed. A woman's breast size can be increased and if she fails to reach orgasm she can be hypnotised into being able to have one. In fact it is possible to talk a woman into an orgasm. Sexual arousal for women is mainly something that takes place primarily in the mind. She imagines the act before doing it and it turns her on. Men can overcome impotence and premature ejaculation. Both *seemingly* physiological problems. *Just because there is an outwardly physiological problem do not assume the cause is not psychological.* The mind affects the body and vice versa.

Words are very powerful – more powerful than

you may hitherto have appreciated. By the way talking to someone about what their subconscious does for them may well induce hypnosis or trance or both.

The subconscious or unconscious is just a term used to refer to a huge variety of processes that occur outside of conscious awareness.

What are you habitually paying attention to?

I remember when I was younger earning money by delivering leaflets for a company that repaired bay windows. This is a very specific type of wooden framed windows. No one really has them anymore. So I would trek up and down streets in my town looking for houses with these old fashioned looking window frames. I had never in my life noticed these things on anyone's houses. I had them on my childhood home: but I never knew that they were bay windows. All of a sudden I was noticing the things everywhere!

It's similar to when I first started wearing glasses: I went outside the opticians and started noticing all these other four-eyed twits like me! The universe is bombarding our senses with data constantly. We cannot consciously process it all: our subconscious mind can. It is aware of billions upon billions upon billions of pieces of information. It passes through to consciousness that which needs to be focused on temporarily until something else 'grabs our attention.'

Plumbers will notice everyone's plumbing, people like me see clinically obese people and wonder what things are missing in their lives that make them eat so much!

News reports focus your attention and prioritise what you are supposed to find important or not. Pain focuses your attention and says: 'Injury! Take care! Get me fixed!' In sport, athletes often focus on targets. *When we focus our attention therefore we are saying **this** is important **that** is not.* There is a rule of mind which says: **you get more of what you focus on**. It is actually quite true. Our normal waking states are focused externally. When we focus internally we are in trance, although people can have eyes wide open and be deeply hypnotised. I would say about 98% of the general public exist in a waking trance state of varying degrees. So don't worry about whether you can hypnotise clients: most are already half way there!

Images of sex and violence grab our attention, they fixate it. Hollywood thrives on creating such images for public consumption. Things out of the ordinary fixate our attention. Consider the sentence, 'I went to the balloon hole.' Balloon hole??! What's a balloon hole? Nothing but it arrested your attention because it was odd. Our brain is fixated when we are afraid. It is looking out for danger, ways to escape etc. By the way your brain is always looking out for potential danger at an unconscious level.

However this 'danger search' can be switched off if we are fixated on something to the exclusion of everything else: what am I talking about? Mobile phones, I-phones and other assorted junk. How many people do you see crossing roads while fixated on those phones? How many girls are oblivious to anything going on around them while texting, checking messages: seeing how 'popular' they are on Facebook?

Look at any commuter train; they are filled with people 'attached,' fixated hypnotically on their phones! If you watch TV (hypnosis), look at the Internet (hypnosis), play computer games (hypnosis), look at your mobile phone with all its pointless apps (hypnosis) when and for how long are you actually awake? What real things are you doing in the real world with real people? For most people under 50 these days the answer is alarmingly, not much. If you are asleep half your life, in trance half your waking life: that's at most a small fraction of life in which you are awake. The more people enter trance states the more people's brain's spontaneously go into them! If you are semi-unconscious for most of your life you are not thinking, you are not conscious, you are a 'trance zombie!' Some hypnotists use the term 'trance junkie.'

Brains which are not used start to atrophy from lack of use. As too your muscles become weak if you don't exercise. *The more time you spend in trance states the more suggestible in general you become.*

Many websites offer hundreds of hypnosis products and suggest you buy lots of them. Wrong. You should enter therapeutic trance rarely. In and out: do the job, then back to waking consciousness. Hypnotic states should be kept pure and untainted. *The aim of good hypnosis is not to go to sleep, it's to wake up.*

Using fruity language will get someone's attention. 'I was going down the road and a f&£"!ing idiot swerved his car toward me!' Now you noticed the f-ing bit, so to speak. Occasionally, rarely throwing in the odd swear word with a client is a good thing. Only with people with whom it is appropriate: you can say,

'Stress makes you feel crappy.'

But don't be a potty mouth, it's unprofessional. It can humanise the process, make you look less of an 'authority figure' when used with precision and create humour too. Humour grabs the attention and is deeply therapeutic too. Trust me some clients will swear. You are matching those ones. They feel you have 'something,' some outlook, perspective in common.

Embedded commands and subliminals.

There is a lot of fuss about the use of so called 'embedded commands.' People imagine they have magical power! They are not commands, they are suggestions. Their purpose is to bypass the critical, analytical conscious mind with all its learnt biases and social programming to be able to speak directly to the subconscious.

In English there are two – only two linguistic structures: statements and questions. There is a variant of statements known as a 'command'. A 'command' is a statement to do something – a direction. It is either an order or a suggestion. No one has to follow a suggestion unless they want to.

A 'mand' is a directive – command, demand, reprimand, countermand etc.

When making a 'command'-suggestion make sure that your tonality goes down at the end of a statement. When asking a question you raise the tone at the end of a sentence. Students and young people have gotten into the habit of never making statements but semi-permanently using a question tone, such as 'I like fish(?)' It is as though they are constantly seeking approval and consensus: it is weak. Make statements that sound like statements and you will sound confident, assertive; as if you know what you are talking about.

Now how do you use imperceptible suggestions with someone you want to hypnotise? You hide them within longer sentences or you simply make the whole sentence sound like a command. By the way statements are just neutral in tone, they stay consistent throughout – the same tone neither rising of falling. But we don't want to make a statement we want to give a helpful suggestion. Now let's just take something such as getting a client to relax. Not necessary in hypnosis but very pleasant and helpful as most people are living lives with unusually and unhealthily high levels of stress. You could say something like this...

*'Now, in order to **'go into trance'** some people find it helpful to **'relax.'***

Very simple, and *conversational* – the embedded suggestions are triple highlighted obviously. The whole thing is very easy, sounds like a normal conversation and allows you to speak directly to the subconscious. How does the subconscious pick up on the idea you'd like it to act on? Well it can hear every single nuance of tone, inflection, melody, accent, rhythm and every other quality of voice you can imagine. It does it all for you outside of your awareness unless you need or want to notice those things for some purposeful reason. Remember people's voice tone may communicate the opposite of what's said in literal terms. In acting this is called 'subtext.'

The subconscious knows how to go into trance and how to relax, it's one of the many things it does for you. When it hears these hidden suggestions and *if it feels so inclined* it will act upon them automatically and independently of conscious mentation. It knows what to do – that works massively in your favour!

In a way it is a form of verbal 'subliminal' (below the threshold of conscious awareness) suggestion, however within the context of helping someone with hypnosis it is acceptable. Why? Subliminals used in advertising are covert manipulation to sell things people don't need. They are coercive, they are attempts at a form of mind control – and they do work. Not on everyone but enough. Bypassing 'conscious sets' during hypnotherapy work is justified – it is often the person's conscious sets that have kept them stuck and unhappy; remember: *conscious and unconscious beliefs may be totally different!* Hidden suggestions are the equivalent of speaking to the organ grinder rather than the monkey. Use them, they work. I will show you how later on and in book 2, on precision language use extensively.

How to get genuine trust.

Remember: *People won't let you hypnotise them if they don't trust you.* Many hypnosis teachers teach what they call 'gaining rapport.' Rapport is taught as being a version of slightly mimicking someone's movement and gestures. Some people call this 'matching and mirroring.' If done at all it should be hyper-subtle and have a time lag. Never exactly copy but do something similar (called 'cross-over matching': they scratch an ear you brush imaginary fluff off your knee) and about 3-5 seconds after they did it. *Most hypnotists are perceived as creepy* and with good reason – most are. Most are perceived as being weird – with good reason; many are weird and hold bizarre beliefs.

The best way to genuinely get someone's trust – the hypnotee (hypnotic subject) – that is the person you are to hypnotise is to act in a friendly, genuine, kindly, appropriate and professional manner. Do not be over friendly, do not pry. The person you are helping is often a complete stranger, respect that.

Most importantly - *you must know exactly what you are doing* – that is you must have exactly the knowledge required to get a client results. This will give you a quiet and comfortable certainty and so set your client at ease. No need for brashness or arrogance. You don't have any hypnotic power. The certainty of knowledge will give you confidence in the desired results.

Another very important thing, the one quality you must have in order to successfully lead someone into a hypnotic experience is *to be the kind of person who genuinely cares for others* – when you are that kind of person others will pick up on it and relax. This does not mean you like everyone you meet. But you at least need to care that your client gets what they are paying for. If you don't the client will know – they are not that stupid. When you open the door to meet a client smile genuinely and offer your hand to shake (if appropriate in your or their culture obviously), say,

'Hello (client's name)? Nice to meet you, please come in.'

As they step into your office, house etc. you have your first act of 'compliance,' that is the first suggestion that you will offer – '...please come in.' As they do step inside you have had one suggestion followed and it seems natural because we all say stuff like that. Suggestions are built up by compounding them. One atop another – each one followed, leading to 'willing compliance.'

Never act lordly high status. Act confident yet low key, as if you are a person who just happens to know lots about hypnosis. It's just a fact. Act in no way as if you are a 'Hypnotist!' with a capital H and an exclamation mark. If your *client* wants to act high-status let them, just be yourself, some people especially in England with its still Indian-like caste system are obsessed with accent, status and social hierarchy as they perceive it. Do not enter into or play this game, it is 'real' in its way but it is a game. As the hypnotist you have all the power and authority in the situation. So don't reveal that, it is just so. If you have someone who is a manager in an office for example they may well act as if because they are 'important' in one context they must act high status in all contexts. Let them play their silly games. Remain confident and calm and assured of your quiet unassuming authority.

Remember: ***you have what they need.*** Never act desperate for someone's money. There are plenty more clients out there.

Remember: rapport is something non-psychopaths do naturally anyway. You were born empathetic of others. You don't need to do visualisations or any other nonsense that some people teach. You were born with the instinctive ability to connect with others. When you do the things I have outlined, even very nervous clients will relax and genuinely trust you.

If you want to be hypnotic be vague.

Vagueness is hypnotic. If you can avoid being specific, concrete or referring to anything in particular - you will send people into trance. Why? _In order to be vague you must talk about things in general terms, when you do you allow the listener/reader to fill in the 'gaps.'_ By so doing they must use their imagination; by using their imagination they enter trance and a light state of hypnosis. Let me give a very simple example:

'I saw a cat.'

Where did I see it? When did I see it? What type of cat was it? Was it a nice cat? Get the idea? We do this in ordinary conversation all the time. In inducing hypnosis you would use vague words in a manner more like this:

'As you sit there,
Wondering what will shift and change first,
You could just draw your attention to your breathing...
Or notice a pleasant sensation inside...
Perhaps in that hand...
Perhaps in that foot,
Maybe in a big toe...
And you know which toe...
because

You know your toes,
you know?'

Nothing specific is said, nobody is told, 'Do this, do that,' but in a vague way you are having your attention redirected through *process language*. This is called 'hypnotic languaging.'

Another example:

'Some people find that that wonderful feeling of relaxation begins to spread.'

Which people? What do you mean by relaxation? Starting and spreading where? Another:

'Everyone goes into trance sooner or later.'

A truism but when specifically? Well at some point – the sentence assumes that trance will happen eventually. Which it will – it is however suggestive to the subconscious that *right now* would be a pretty good idea. See how simple it is? How simple what is?!!! Ok that's enough of that for now...

If you want to be hypnotic use truisms.

If you say things that are obviously true a person's critical faculty 'relaxes,' it doesn't analyse incoming data and so that person becomes more open to suggestion – note I said *more open* not a programmable idiot. Let me show you what I mean.

'Change is possible.'

'In some situations you'd like to feel more confident.'

'There are improvements that can be made in your health, wealth and relationships.'

These are the kind of 'cold reading' generalisations that fake psychics use. They are so general they apply to 99.9% of humans on planet earth. In hypnosis some good truisms are:

'You are sitting there...' **(verifiable fact.)** *wondering just exactly how this will happen...* **(assumed mind reading/guessing)** *you are breathing in the way you are...* **(verifiable – they are breathing)** *you can notice certain sensations...* **(verifiable otherwise they'd be dead)** *Perhaps the most pleasant one can captivate*

you? Now... **(we can be captivated by nice sensations – this is a suggestion too – you have made some truisms and added on a suggestion which is more likely to be accepted because you said a few truisms in a row.)**

A pattern followed by hypnotists is: fact, fact, fact, suggestion. The above example is called a 'Yes set.' The person's analytical mind effectively says 'Yes, yes, yes to the truisms – then you give a suggestion which is more likely to be followed by another yes. Easy. Remember, and this is a truism – *anyone can learn hypnosis: it is so easy to do.* The fact is you have been doing a lot of this without knowing already, we all use these methods of communication from time to time, we just generally don't use them with conscious awareness, skill or purpose. As you are consciously and unconsciously learning these skills don't be too surprised if you start noticing others using them too. Newsreaders and politicians use them a lot.

Truisms make the analytical filter say, 'No problem,' no beliefs are violated. One of the functions of the conscious mind is to guard you from possibly harmful influences.

If you want to be hypnotic use vividly descriptive language.

'Imagine you are walking through a beautiful forest at the height of summer. The woodland is full of life and abundance. You can feel the rough bark of the trees, the sweet smell of the summer flowers; the sound of a cooling, soothing wind as it eases its way through the tree tops. You stop to enjoy the view; it is a unique and precious moment that will never exist again. You breathe in the clean fresh air before taking a bite out of the most delicious ice cream you have ever tasted.'

Painting pictures with words activates the imagination: *the activation of the imagination is the key to hypnosis and trance.* Use and evoke all the senses not just sight, describe sounds, tastes and smells. Great fiction writing is deeply hypnotic. If the book 'captures your imagination' so that you are *fully absorbed* in the imaginative life of the author's characters, feeling their emotions and identifying with them and their predicament then you are hypnotised, quite literally, by the book.

Words to stimulate the imagination.

On their own the following words immediately demand the activation of the imagination and so instantly elicit a hypnotic response:

Imagine...
Picture...
Visualise
What if...
I have a vision of... (a politician's favourite.)
What would it be like if...
See in your mind's eye...
Suppose...
Pretend (the word all children use when starting a game.)

Get the imagination of the person you want to hypnotise activated and you are half way home...next...

You *never* need to use a convincer to get results.

Many hypnotists advise that you NEED a 'hypnotic convincer' to get change in someone. Nonsense. It is entirely unnecessary to elicit trance, hypnosis or get therapeutic change. You may well have an individual whose hand you can stick to their leg, whose hand lifts and rests in mid-air. It doesn't mean that they will stop smoking, lose weight etc. as a result. It won't add to the effectiveness of the change work, if you are doing any that is. *The best 'convincer' is that the person being hypnotised feels that they are hypnotised.* When they get that feeling they will know that someone is going to happen – most of the time. Later on in this book I'll show you a worthwhile 'convincer.'

Is there such a thing as hypnotic talent?

Yes but anyone can be taught given enough time to enter a wonderful state of hypnosis. It 'seems' (and I stress the word seems) that highly creative and intelligent people make the best hypnotic subjects, I have also noted an ability to use abstract thought and to think in terms of symbols as indicative of good subjects. I will explain this more in a later book. Some people are so primed to experience hypnosis that they will go into it even before you start a formal induction.

There is some research that suggests that the ability to dissociate is genetic. There is some research that children brought up in environments where creative play was encouraged find it easier to enter trance and hypnotic states; however in my experience *all sufficiently motivated people can experience a therapeutic trance.*

Factors that may prevent a person entering trance are extreme anxiety, a perceived loss of status, a person who is overly concerned with the idea of control. Also subjects who have encountered incompetent hypnotists or therapists who hypnotised them and forced their own ideas of what was good for a client on them may have problems trusting other hypnotists. There are too many incompetent people claiming to be hypnotists: the worst are often very well trained. A rare few subjects will not enter hypnosis because they are playing silly buggers and wasting your time. The best people to work with are the 'hyper-responsive' people; they're fun!

To hypnotise someone get them to 'go inside.'

1. In order to get someone into a great state of hypnosis, not just light trance ask them to have their feet flat on the floor, sitting up in a comfy chair, have them place their hands flat down (palm side) on their thighs. Clients can lie down, that's fine but stranger's especially women feel vulnerable sometimes if even offered the option.

2. To ensure that their head is supported so they don't get a neck ache (use cushions, pillows if you have to; they will be so relaxed if they don't support their head they might be in agony on awakening!)

3. Say, *'Ok just close your eyes and just pay attention to any sensations inside that you usually ignore...'*

In that one sentence you have the beginnings of hypnosis. Now in what other ways do we all 'go inside'?

We remember things.
We imagine things.
We project possible futures.

We fantasise.
We notice internal sensations such as when we need to go to the toilet, the feeling of comfort after a nice meal.

So let's form a mock induction with these facts in mind.

'Close your eyes and just pay attention to where you already feel most comfort...
As you do, perhaps you can notice any pleasant memories that come to mind...
Maybe a happy time...
It's possible you might ponder what kind of change you want...
And it can be secret change...
Can you notice how your comfort has already increased?
Which hand is lighter than the other, which hand is warmer?'

All of the above direct a person's attention internally. To get an intense state of hypnosis in which your client's will have the best time and get the best results, they'll get that by going inside and recognising the things you point out. It doesn't even seem like hypnosis, you are almost just pointing out facts: who wants to resist a fact? By the way 99.9% of the time client's won't resist going into hypnosis: it just feel so wonderful! Most people prefer trance to being awake. Don't believe me? Go into a shopping mall. Now how many people really seem awake to you? If any? Most people are in a state of trance from dolly daydream to pathological trance. My best friend's mum calls such people 'farts in trances.'

Introspection is hypnosis.

Ask someone to close their eyes, go inside and imagine arranging a bunch of flowers lying on a table in a vase. In order to do this they must enter hypnosis; introspection is hypnosis.

Words that focus attention.

To hypnotise someone you need to 'lock' someone's attention in. How?

Focus...*on my voice...*
Pay attention to x...*your breathing.*
Become aware of...*where you feel most calm.*
Notice...*how your breathing has changed; such changes are standard.*
Stop! *And just relax...*
Stare at that spot/candle...*and allow your eyelids to begin to feel heavier and heavier...*
Look into my eyes...*(stage hypnotist favourite.)*
Look...*the new budget will be delivered on time...(politician's favourite. It's a command to* look *at them!)*
Listen...*to these words.*
Where do you feel x? *Most comfortable etc.*
Locate that feeling...*inside.*
Exactly where do you see that image?

These words and phrases will begin the process of hypnosis.

How to have a good 'hypnotic voice.'

A good 'hypnotic voice' is one that is able to be modulated well. It has variety. Monotone hypnotic voices work but there is a much more powerful way to speak to achieve your ends. The tone, speed, rhythm and many other vocal factors will help you help your clients to achieve many of their desired goals. My women clients often compliment me on my voice. Unlike most hypnotists however I am also a trained actor.

Some hypnotists say that using a 'hypno-voice' sounds awful and is unnecessary. It is true that you can hypnotise someone in your normal speaking voice. I will explain why that is an inane idea. Your hypnotic voice should be relaxing, smooth and resonant.

1. The voice should resonate in the chest, not the throat and especially not the nose!

2. The voice should be given power and energy from the diaphragm.

3. The voice should be slightly quieter than your normal speaking voice.

4. The voice should be somewhat slower but not too much. A few pauses...now

and again...can help...to allow people to...process your suggestions. But don't overdo it.

The best way to get the right hypnotic tone is to think about this: *when you speak to another person you are literally bathing them in sound.* Your sound. How do you feel if an authority figure shouts at you? Not the right tone for hypnosis. How would you lull a baby to sleep? If you want to calm someone else down what do you do? That's right; you speak in a calm, relaxed tone. You slow down somewhat. You speak deliberately and clearly. Imagine that your voice actually affects a listener's neurology because it does. Powerfully.

I think it is best to have at least 3 hypnotic voices: one for light hypnotic trance, two for medium hypnotic trance, three for very deep hypnotic trance. As you take a client deeper, slow...down more...deepen your voice more...speak even more resonantly. I'll explain resonance in a bit.

Speak to a client as though what you have to say is important, because it is. *The hypnotic state has the effect of making your words seem significant, imbued with a deep meaning and purpose.* Your 'waking up voice' should be quicker, higher pitched (not squeaky or shrill think 'lighter,' not so intense a way of speaking) and more energised.

If you want someone to feel confident say it in a confident tone. If you want someone to feel happy, say it in a happy tone. If you want someone to be able to access their sense of humour more often: a highly essential life skill, then put a teeny bit of a giggle in your voice. This is called varying your intonation.
Some hypnotists like to use a kind 'motherly voice,' some like the slightly sterner 'fatherly voice.' A combination of the two is best. Kind but authoritative rather than authoritarian with a light touch.

Use your normal voice for the waking state.
Use a relaxed voice for inducing trance.
Use a deeper tone for speaking to the subconscious.
Use an even deeper tone for the unconscious.

Why? Because when you use these different tones you condition a client to associate that tone with that mental state. So guess what happens? The client can go into a trance after a few sessions just by you using that voice tone. If you use your waking voice for all stages of the hypnotic process what will happen? You don't want clients to associate your normal voice with trance do you?

Remember as a hypnotist your voice is your tool for being able to work at all. Look after it. Hypnosis demands a bit of the performer in us, you will and should be using your voice as a trained actor would, knowing how each intonation and shift of pace will purposefully affect a client. Squeeze the meaning out of your words. A glass of water nearby for a dry throat is a handy thing for a hypnotist to have. A hypnotist is a public speaker; albeit usually he or she has an audience of one!

If you think public speaking classes or actor training/voice coaching would help then avail yourself of them. A good book on how to improve your voice is,
'Your voice and how to enrich it for speaking, acting and everyday conversation,' by Andrew Armitage.
It is a very simple and easy to follow book for beginners up. There are many books on professional use of the voice, checking out Amazon for all its titles on the subject might be a good idea.

You are your voice. How good is yours? How good could it be? Most people use their voice crudely. You will have an advantage over competitors by having a good voice.

I will leave you with a tip to boost your voice's

strength and power; here it comes, are you ready? Hum. Just gently hum. Do it now and again and soon your will have more vocal power.

As an interesting note: the human voice can trigger an ASMR response: Autonomous Sensory Meridian Response – aka 'head tingles,' 'brain orgasm.'

Resonance – think Barry White, that deep, chesty growl like quality. Think a lion's roar or a bear's for that matter. It suggests power. When resonance is 'placed' in the chest it sounds nicer to the human ear.

An exercise for a more resonant voice.

1. Breath out *slowly* till all breath is expelled. Do it slowly so you don't get dizzy. If you get dizzy look at your open hand held directly in front of your face.
2. Allow yourself to *'breathe into your stomach'* which will expand; when your tummy expands it means you are breathing with your diaphragm. This is the correct way to breath: anxious people and people with weak voices breathe at the top of their chest. When you breathe via the diaphragm your voice is 'supported.' An unsupported voice is one that has run out of breath. Breathe out all your

breath and speak to see what I mean.

3.   Now, when you tummy is 'full' of air, slowly release it on a hum. Keep the note in your vocal range.

4.   You have resonators in your chest, throat, front of mouth, nasal cavity and forehead.

5.   Direct the hum to these various resonators. Remember: for hypnosis you want a nice chest resonance.

6.   Experiment how each resonating 'chamber' affects the sound you make.

7.   As an interesting note different areas, countries and cultures use differing resonators as part of the local dialect. Liverpudlians have a nasal tendency as do people from Northern Ireland.

Solar plexus breathing.

If you want to hypnotise someone, get them to imagine that they are breathing through their solar plexus. This is the spot at the base of your breastbone, the small indentation at the top of your tummy, the bottom centre of your chest, pecs, boobs. You can feel the dip there with your hand. Now this area is said to contain huge nerve bundles. Clients often report feelings emanating from this point. When you simply say,

'Just imagine that you are breathing through your solar plexus.'

you'll start to get someone to go deeper. That's all you have to say; when people do this their breathing very quickly becomes more relaxed and soon it becomes hypnotic breathing. There is a breathing pattern for people in hypnosis. It becomes almost unnoticeable – the in breath is very small, very slight. You'll notice the tummy hardly rises. Notice how hypnosis is about giving a client a long series of small tasks: together these tasks create hypnotic trance.

I have no idea why this works but it does. I suggest you use it during inductions, especially the first time you hypnotise a given individual.

Use the client's name: a lot!

People like hearing their own name. Other people don't say it enough. It makes people feel acknowledged and important. Which few people feel these days. Use their name a lot in the interview/chat stage and during hypnosis. Notice how politicians will often ask the person's first name...

'Samantha I agree with you on that point. I sympathise but...'

Think about it this way: in totalitarian states and prisons people are not called by their name but by a number.

The 'doing nothing' pattern.

At the very beginning of a hypnosis session you can say something like this...

'For the duration of this process, there is nowhere for you to go, nothing for you to do...'

This covers everything. It says: you don't have to think, worry, work or do anything at all. In hypnosis and trance that's what people do – nothing! At least not from the outside, inside there is much activity occurring. It's a time to rest and relax.

Deconstructing a hypnosis script.

Ok totally copyright free, for personal use that is, I am letting you have this script which I created for nothing. I am going to give you my 99.9% successful hypnosis script: it works on everyone unless they are some kind of twit!

The full un-annotated script is in the appendix. You can work from that one to practise. At this stage you are analysing things to learn the core hypnotic principles: the basics if you like.

The italicised text is what I would say to a client, highlighted parts are embedded commands and underneath the segment of the script is an analysis of what I am doing. I call it simply my 'basic induction': I use it with clients for their first session. For 99.9% that's usually enough...

One final thing, some of the language patterns used are not covered in this book, you'll have to read my second book on precision language use. I don't want you to be overwhelmed with too much info at this stage. But you don't need to know about them in order for the script to work very well for you. Without further ado...

The Rogue Hypnotist's Basic Induction.

'Ok just close your eyes...
It is now time to **feel growing comfort**...'
(It is now time = something different is about
to happen + embedded command 'feel growing
comfort.')
_'You don't have to do anything else, just simply
pay attention to your breathing...'_
(The 'You don't have to' pattern plus 'Not doing
pattern.' 'Just simply' = only do this i.e. focus
plus adverb – simply, that is it's not
complicated. 'Just simply' also softens the
command – 'pay attention to your breathing.'
Attention is being focused inside. By the way let
them focus on their breathing for about 5-7
seconds)
_'And now, as you do, take a deep breath and
hold it for a moment, that's right, and just **let
go** as you slowly release that breath and
relax...'_
('And now' pattern – something is about to
happen! 'As you do' = unspecified verb – as you
do what? Confusing and vague. Next is the
command – 'take a deep breath and hold it.' I
am taking control of an unconscious response –
breathing and altering it. Make sure they hold
that breath! Just for a second or two. 'That's
right' = encouragement for following
instructions. Some hypnotists think that if
someone follows instructions that's hypnosis: I

think it's more complicated. 'And just' =
softener and limited function – only, just.
Embedded command 'let go'; '...as you slowly' =
adverb – I'm telling them exactly how to
breathe out and also a slow out breathe induces
relaxation. Finally: 'and relax' = embedded
command – 'relax.' See how much I've done in
just the first few sentences! They have no
chance – too much is going on – consciousness
gives up and goes into trance. You have
overwhelmed it!)

*'And again – deep breath in and slowly release
that breath and just* **relax a bit more**...*'*
(Hopefully getting self-explanatory – repetition
and narrowed focus plus compounding
suggestions. Ending with embed.)

'When you relax on an out breath – **your
comfort only increases**...*that's right...'*
(Lots going on here – truism - 'when you relax
on an out breath etc.' – but Holmes however
did you deduce it?! Embed is also a
presupposition, it assumes comfort is already
there.)

*'You don't have to do anything at all...nowhere
to go...nothing to do as you* **go into trance**...*'*
('Do nothing' pattern and first obvious and clear
hypnotic embed 'go into trance.')

*'Noticing any pleasant sensations, processes,
experiences as you* **go inside, now**...*'*
(Narrow focus of attention on 'internal
processes' which are left totally unspecified –

the client fills the gaps – 'sensations, processes, experiences' – meaningless drivel unless you are a hypnotist then it becomes a 'super suggestion.' 'Go inside' is a direct embed for trance.)

'Because all you need to do as you just allow certain things to happen...'

('Because' = a word that gives a fake solidity, a seeming reason to do the next thing. 'You' = conscious mind. 'Allow certain things etc.' – what things???! It implies something hypnotic due to the context and something independent of conscious volition too!)

'...is to turn your attention inward and become aware of things occurring in your body...'

(Command – focus inwardly. Become aware of body = internal body focus.)

'And recognise and experience any reactions within that body to these words...'

(Non-specified verb – 'recognise' – what does that mean?? 'Any reactions...??' - presupposes there will be reactions, which ones? Who knows! 'That body' = conscious and unconscious dissociation. 'These words' = which words? And presupposes that my words are powerful enough to induce unconscious reactions. Can you see how many multi-layered suggestions the poor sucker of a client is faced with and all so subtly? No chance of escape!)

'And be able to feel how good they feel as you **feel, really feel a kind of comfort***...'*

('Feel how good they feel etc.' = mild confusion, lots of *feels* in there and finalising this hypnotic paragraph off with another suggestion of comfort that they can *really* feel.)
'Imagine breathing through your solar plexus..'
(Direct command plus hypnotic word 'imagine' to start activating the imagination. A note on breathing: if a client starts trying to consciously alter their breathing, holding it in too long and breathing out loudly through the lips say something like, 'Thanks but you don't have to do anything to your breathing just let the changes happen naturally.' Obviously we are using the solar plexus breathing pattern here.)
*'Now, imagine a colour that makes you **feel very calm and comfortable, now**...'*
('Now' = command for client to follow previous command. 'Imagine a colour' = direct command, evoking imagination – 'colour feelings' pattern (see the next book). Colours being used for first time – this entails visualisation which is hypnotic plus I am leaving it up to them to imagine their own relaxing colour – who knows maybe black, gold or purple relaxes them, don't assume blue and green relaxes everyone. 'Makes' = fake cause and effect – why does imagining a colour 'make' you relax? Because I just said it did, this is an example of 'trance logic': it seems plausible yet is actually gibberish! I end up with a another embed for feeling calm and comfortable;

feelings evoked, an unconscious response plus feeling calm and comfy makes them feel good and allows them to learn more easily. Make the experience as lovely as you can for someone: I gradually escalate the level of feeling – comfort, more comfort, very comfortable! Sentence ends on another 'now' – a command to do it now...)

'Allow a wave of that colour of comfort to begin to spread from the top of your head, all the way down, to the tips of your toes...'

('Allow' = don't do it consciously! 'A wave' = suggesting waves of feelings seems to do wonders, I have no idea why; you can say things like, *'You can feel wave after wave of absolutely wonderful feelings, awesome feelings spreading throughout your body, making you feel fantastic!'* 'Begin to spread' i.e. we haven't even got started yet! Basically this sentence is a fairly explicit command to experience very quick full body relaxation; saves you spending ten minutes gradually relaxing each muscle. Notice also the time frame is not specified, so the subconscious can carry on the relaxation till it's satisfied. I also threw in a sneaky 'all the way down' pattern if you noticed? An indirect suggestion to go deeper.)

'All of your muscles becoming softer, letting go now...'

(Self-explanatory by now I hope.)

'...as you notice any sounds you hear, any words that I say, anything and everything

71

*allows your good feelings to only increase, allows you to **drift off**...'*

(This is a suggestion that no matter what happens in the environment it won't disturb the person, in fact it will make them MORE hypnotised! 'Drift off' is a suggestion to daydream: i.e. go into trance. Always add in more good feelings, most people feel rough and stressed on a daily basis and they think it's normal.)

'You are free to wander and wonder...'

(Indirect command to experience trance. It is also ambiguous, phonetically that is, 'wonder/wander' – also suggestive of going on a journey – into the subconscious mind.)

'As you relax even more deeply you can know that the mind and body are one interconnected unit and where the mind leads, the body follows and where the body leads the mind follows..'

(Truism – yes set. Vague and slightly confusing – the listener searches unconsciously for the meaning/s.)

'You may hear the sound of my voice going with you...'

(Indirect command – listen to my voice plus you might drift in and out sometimes hearing my voice, sometimes not. Remember they can't turn their ears off, so the subconscious is listening anyway. 'Going with you' - into? Trance of course – implied.)

'Only pleasant thoughts, pleasant images,

*perhaps one particularly relaxing memory can **drift** through your mind as you fully **enter this state**.'*

(I call this 'shutting down the experience'; I don't want the client to access unpleasant ideas, thoughts, images, traumas etc. I want it to ONLY be a nice experience. No pain no gain is for idiots, masochists and sadists. We want pleasurable change. Notice I leave them to choose what will happen – 'pleasant images' or thoughts or a memory – it's up to them. I set up a framework – that's all. 'Drift' again is suggestive of floating – hypnosis feels 'floaty' to some – and of trance. We also drift into sleep. 'Enter this state' – which state? Could be hypnosis, relaxation, trance – anything.)

'You don't have to open your eyes or talk, let me do the talking for a while...'

(This is directly from Milton Erickson – an indirect command to: *shut up!* Stop talking on the inside. This is done through implication – the 'you don't have to' pattern. The client was talking during the interview stage now it's time to quieten down.)

'Do you really think you are awake?'

(This is a subtle challenge, it also implies: you are hypnotised - aren't you? This is also from Erickson – note: do not use it if your client is a contrarian – they might wake up to spite you. This one is an option – it is a good deepener.)

'You don't have to understand consciously, your

beliefs, your unconscious beliefs are all that matters.'

(Truism – the unconscious mind is in charge, consciousness is limited and unable to solve the problem, that's why the client is there with you seeking help. Conscious understanding won't solve the problem. It also implies a conflict up to that point is about to be resolved.)

'Which part is most comfortable?'

('Part?' – leg, foot, mind, body? Who knows? Presupposes comfort again. Remember *hypnosis feels comfortable*. Suggestive of change.)

*'Funny to find **all feels well**...'*

('Funny...' – surprise, humour, folk language - an unconscious response plus an embed suggestive of how we comfort children – 'all better.')

'On occasion it can be very good and pleasant enjoying letting go of certain directions and controls to permit unconscious autonomous/independent processes to take over...'

(Truism/generalisation – 'certain directions and controls'; conscious mind basically with its functions and biases. Also suggestive that the subconscious knows much more than the conscious, which it does. 'Unconscious autonomous/independent processes etc.' – use autonomous for well-read/educated people, independent for others. This is basically saying we let the unconscious do lots of things for us that are beneficial – sleep, digest food, be creative, dream, orgasm and other wonderful feelings and of course hypnosis! A reassurance that it's safe to 'let go.' Two more paragraphs left...)

'You may be wondering what will shift and change first...'

('Wonder' = a hypnotic word plus presupposition that a change of some sort will happen; it is also only one of many...)

'And you can easily use all your powers of imagination, intelligence and inner focus ensuring you will achieve all you desire from this session without knowing how you did it consciously...'

(Ok, 'easily' - adverb, the change will be easy. Change isn't hard when you know how; use lots of words that presuppose ease, effortlessness etc. 'Use all your powers etc...' = the client does the work not you! Throw them on their resources to self-heal. You do need to use imagination, intelligence and concentration for hypnosis to work – a truism. Statement command – 'you will achieve etc...' 'Without knowing how you etc...' = the change will occur unconsciously.)

'How much further into trance and hypnosis can you really go?'

(Presupposition deepener – implies you are in trance already, now go deeper – indirect

command.)
'Enjoy feeling more and more comfortable as you go deeper inside...'
(Directionalising process toward comfort with false linkage – 'as you' – go deeper. You can embed words like 'comfort', 'relax,' 'calm': all by themselves. The subconscious is well aware how to 'do' calmness, relaxation etc. These words act as triggers to elicit the state. Also notice partial use of 'the more the more' pattern. See book two for details.)
'You could notice words and notice noticing words...'
('You could' – it's possible, you don't have to but you could plus gentle, poetic like confusion, 'notice noticing.')
'And the deeper you go, the more wonderful you feel and the more wonderful you feel the deeper you can go, now...that's right!'
(Super command – 'deeper you go etc.' I first learnt this from a top UK stage hypnotist. It just works beautifully and is probably the deftest linguistic deepener there is. It uses 'the more the more' pattern, mild confusion and links going deeper with feeling not just good but wonderful. No one resists this – who doesn't want to feel wonderful!?)
*'As we continue you can **hear my voice** and at other times it might seem quiet or distant and at other times it doesn't matter if you can hear it at all because you can allow a deeper part of*

you to hear all you need to hear, here/hear and now...'

('As we continue...' – pronoun we = me and client, emphasising that it's a collaborative effort. I am the guide only. 'Hear my voice' embed – listen to me! Also I give all possible alternatives (alter-natives!!): the list that follows are all truisms – some clients just focus on your voice, some drift off into la-la land, others have the bizarre experience that the hypnotist has moved far away. 'Here/hear' = phonetic ambiguity – notice my confusion technique is gentle and poetic not harsh. 'Deeper part' – subconscious, unconscious, Fred, Sarah who knows! Even when asleep we can't turn our ears off – something is listening.)

'You know that you are the one who is in control as we make even more amazing changes.'

('You know' – 'mind reading' pattern. 'You are the one in control' – cede control to the client – you are the guide, the facilitator of change only. The unconscious knows specifically what has to change – you don't. During the hypnotic process do not be afraid to pause for between 5 to 10 seconds to let these suggestions sink in. I will occasionally say stuff like,

'And you can process that while I'm quiet...'
And/or,
'You can process that in the pause/pores...'
I quite like the pause/pores ambiguity because

it is suggestive of deep-rooted change.)
'And anyone can feel confident each day…'
(Anyone? = <u>you</u> dummy! You can start giving therapeutic suggestions during the induction. You should have been 'idea seeding' even earlier. I'll show you specifically how further on in the series of books.)
'And you can follow your own associative processes to these words, can you not? Like the word 'comfort' and follow where it leads you…now…'
(Remember: <u>*words are symbols*</u> – the human mind works via symbols, often images are symbols of something, they do not exist in a meaningless context. Also you are triggering an internal search for meaning – the so-called 'trans-derivational' search of NLP. We often follow associational chains of thought. 'Comfort' is a good chain of thought to follow in trance. Notice also the tag question – 'can you not?' Hiding commands in pseudo questions is a good trick. We are almost done.)
*'Your eyelid muscles can feel so relaxed that you '**eyes**' easily remain '**closed**' and as they do you feel even more absorbed in pleasant processes…'*
(Ok folks I lied, I am doing a little bit of a convincer – an eye closure/catalepsy one. I am using the 'hypnotic coding' pattern – notice 'eyes closed' is the command but hidden, separated and linked only by your command

tonality. 'Absorbed in pleasant processes,' who even has the foggiest as to what this means? Works though; an example of hypno-gibberish. Hypno-speak is often meaningful sounding nonsense. Reading nonsense poetry might help.)

'Each out breath helps melt past tension which floats away into the distance like storm clouds melting, fading away in the sunshine guaranteeing your success...'

(Linking breathing out with relaxation – a truism and therapeutic; remember your clients are so habitually tense, it does them good. Metaphor/imagery – comparing tension to storm clouds and sunshine with success. These types of metaphors are globally relevant. Also false linkage between success therapeutically and relaxing. There is no cause effect relationship but you just suggested there is.)

'Knowing you don't have to do those things you once did...'

('Knowing!!!?' Who knows?? 'You don't have to etc.,' = 'don't have to' pattern plus 'do those things you once did,' = indirect command to change habits; also a truism. They don't HAVE to do the things like over eating, watching porn, staying awake – whatever they once did. You imply choice.)

'As a person's mind develops other awareness's, ***the body can...rest***...'

('A person' - obviously being the client – it is

dissociative language too. Here I am asking the mind and body to dissociate. Also throwing in a 'rest' embed is good therapeutically; having problems is tiring. Also when we rest we can? Recover!)

'...You don't have to move unless that movement brings you more of that which you wish...'

(Hypno-babble! Basically – don't move, sit still and only move to get more comfy. We are done. We haven't even added a 'formal' deepener yet...Can you see how seemingly innocuous words can have such multiple meanings?!)

By this stage your clients are hypnotised, they are focused inside; later in this book I'll show you how to deepen the state.

The moment of hypnotic surrender.

In ALL hypnotic inductions there comes the point where the conscious mind 'gives up,' let's go and hypnosis takes place. It is my opinion that this occurs because hypnosis is so pleasurable. By letting go, the beginnings of that foretaste of pleasure are surrendered to. Hypnosis just feels so damn good to people that they eventually let go and go into la-la land.

You will detect this moment easily: the person looks inwardly focused, their face is more relaxed; then suddenly all the facial muscles smooth out, the person becomes very still, their head flops or gently rolls to one side, it may do this quickly or slowly. You just know it when you see it. Look out for *the moment of hypnotic surrender,* that's when you can say – GOT YOU! When you see it, verbally reinforce it by saying,

'That's right.'

Elongate the vowel sounds when you do.

Your bonus: Da, da, daaa! The worthwhile convincer!

I very, very rarely do 'convincers': if you think about it logically, dispassionately, doing a convincer implies you doubt what you are doing! The best convincers for clients are therapeutic success; that is, they achieve their goals.

I elicit very pleasurable feelings in people to show them how their subconscious can do this without any effort on their part. Healing should be pleasurable – after all it is about returning to good health. Some highly responsive subjects will overtly display signs of extreme pleasure in their body language. These are the clients who would make great stage hypnosis subjects. Also known as 'somnambulists.' They are hyper hypnotisable. They will easily be able to stick their hands to their leg as if stuck by glue etc. So without further ado...The worthwhile convincer...I actually call it:

The Pleasure Deepener.

(Hypnosis is assumed.)

'Not yet but soon I will count from 1 to 3 and say BLISS!
When I do you can allow yourself to

feel absolutely wonderful for no particular reason.

feeling good...feeling happy...
feeling content, comfortable...
*even **blissful, now,***
better than you have felt for some time.
And when I say DEEPER
you can go 20 times deeper than you were...
and you can feel even better
because the golden rule of hypnosis is
the deeper you go the better you feel
and the better you feel the deeper
you can go, nooow...
Is that ok with you?
Are you ready?
(Don't wait for a response)
Here we go...
1-2-3 BLISS! (say it blissfully)
And that just feels really good doesn't it?
***Feeling really good**...*
DEEPER!
The deeper you go the better you feel
and the better you feel
the deeper you can go...that's right.
And that feels even better doesn't it?
Ok...and again... ('Ok' gets the subconscious ready)
1-2-3 BLI-ISS!!
And that feels even better doesn't it?
feeling really good,
even better than before!

DEEPER!
The deeper you go the better you feel
and the better you feel the deeper you can go!
And that does feel even better doesn't it!
*Just **enjoy these good feelings**...*
That's right...
And one more time for luck...
1-2-3 BLISS!!!
And that feels really good doesn't it?
Whatever that feeling is you're feeling...
perhaps the best feeling so far?
Learning what you need to learn from this
experience...
because your subconscious is the seat
of your emotions...
*it can let you **feel more comfort**,*
more confidence**, **more relaxed alertness
when needed,
bursts of good feelings for no reason...
Even better ones
more and more and more...
and you can, can you not?
DEEPER!
The deeper you go the better you feel...
And the better you feel the deeper you can go...
Nooooowww!
Deeper and deeper into trance and hypnosis!
Deeper than you've ever been before, now.'

(Carry on with session etc.)

Remember your clients are miserable 99% of the time. Give 'em a lift! Be a Blissnotist; do Blissnosis.

Signs of hypnosis and 'response potential.'

How do you know if someone is hypnotised, ready to be hypnotised, entranced? Ok here's a list of thing to look out for. If they occur say,

'That's right...'

You are verbally rewarding the client: conditioning them.

1.   Their face and neck flush with blood. (A woman once did this just before I started an induction formally – her unconscious knew how to go into trance and it began even before I said anything formally hypnotic.)
2.   The face becomes pale.
3.   Physical stillness.
4.   Fidgeting and scratching nose.
5.   Mouth hangs open.
6.   Eyes roll back revealing white of eyes under eyelids. (Not pretty!)
7.   Head rolls or flops downward toward chest.
8.   Head rolls to side.
9.   They start snoring! Like a pig sometimes! People are sometimes worried that they'll snore, it happens, assure them you don't care. It's funny when they do it anyway.
10. They just look peaceful and asleep.
11. The facial muscles smooth out completely

and the face looks a bit like a wax model.

12. Twitching, spasms.

13. Sighing.

14. REM: rapid eye movement; an indication of dreaming. Hypnosis is not REM sleep! It is completely unique and discreet. It just looks like REM sometimes. They might be visualising, talking to themselves, listening to internal sounds. Haven't the foggiest really!

15. The kiss me look – the eyes stare softly straight ahead while still open – the goo goo eyes look; that look a girl gives you before she wants you to kiss her for the first time. Your client's don't want you to kiss them! The eyes widen and pupils dilate (enlarge). This is the 'response potential' look. If someone does this - you got them! Good subjects will do it in the interview stage as you merely tell them something of interest. It is as though they are mesmerised by your conversation. Remember: hypnosis is about teaching people fascinating things.

16. Clients may speak out loud, say names, act as though eating food.

17. Tummy rumble (digestive system relaxes).

18. This is the freakiest one: it happens rarely – I call it 'The Zombie Look'; it is actually quite alarming. Rarely (it has only happened with two women) at the point where deep hypnosis is achieved the person will, with their eyes closed, turn their head toward you and 'stare' at you.

The face looks utterly blank: depersonalised, the conscious personality of the person is gone and just a blank slate remains! No one tells you about this in hypnosis school! The only way to describe it is as though the person's soul is looking at you but the eyes are closed! Weird!!!

19. After a session clients may report that during hypnosis they noticed the following as signs of trance: time distortion (time seemed to pass quickly - an hour may have seemed like 5 minutes), heaviness of limbs and inability to move them (spontaneous catalepsy), feeling as though the hypnotist's voice and or person were far away, inability to open eyelids even after trying. All of these hypnotic phenomena are indictors of natural convincers. They happen naturally so why ask for specific ones? What if the subconscious doesn't want to lift the arm that day? What if it doesn't want to stick a hand to a wall? I just let these happen naturally. I am not a stage hypnotist. I have nothing to prove. I know this stuff works – powerfully. I let the subconscious decide what it wants to do.

Oh yes I almost forgot, clients may report they were bored! That's ok; it's a sign of trance. These spontaneous trance events confirm to the client that something unique did indeed happen – sometimes they say, 'My arms felt heavy,' yet I had given no suggestion for heaviness to occur. Many clients wake up and say, 'That was bizarre/weird!' 'I went on a

journey,' 'Wow!' 'That was intense!' 'I feel tired,'
is also common. Remember they have been
using their brain, not a common thing for a lot
of people! And they have been using its
capacities in ways they hitherto haven't. It can
be tiring.
20. A fixed unblinking stare. Different from goo-
goo eyes. People in eyes open hypnosis have a
fixed, unblinking stare. Watch people watching
TV. Hypnotised! It is quite a harsh look, more
intense than goo-goo eyes.

A woman once said she was afraid she'd start
talking to me in hypnosis, presumably telling
me stuff. Who knows? Definite sign of watching
too much TV and building a model of reality on
fiction. I assured her I had no desire to speak
with her in the hypnosis state. That was that.

Deepeners: all the way down!

The state of hypnosis, when done properly, is relaxing but intense. The intensity of the state is deepened by hypnotic deepeners. I will teach you how to construct your own deepeners in the next book. For now use this very good and short deepener, it's better than the walking down the stairs one. By the way using my method you will encounter people who were hypnotised before who will say, it didn't feel like that last time. What I teach is much more intense, it's a no ifs or buts state, people like it. It is true hypnosis! I call it a state of *pure hypnosis*.

The Magic Wall deepener.

'See a wall in your mind's eye...
In a moment, not yet but soon,
you'll see numbers going downward from 20-1.
they will appear on that wall.
they'll be a certain helpful colour.
As I count down from 20-1
those numbers will change,
to match the numbers
I am counting **downward now***,*
all the way down,
and as they head towards 1
they'll shrink
increasingly so,

like those things in Alice in Wonderland
that changed size.
And before they reach 15
they'll have shrunk so small
that they will have disappeared,
vanished;
just like that.
And when that happens
you will already have entered
a profoundly wonderful state
of deep trance and deep hypnosis,
*deep hypnotic **SLEEP!***
Deeper than ever before, now...
Ok, here we go...
20, 19, numbers shrinking...
***going down**...*
18, deeper, smaller...
17, even more so...
16, almost there,
***going all the way down**...*
15! Gone completely!
Vanished!
It's so nice, so pleasing...
is it not?'

Successful deepeners have a formula, read book 2 in the series, 'Mastering hypnotic language,' to discover it. You have two in this book, The Pleasure Deepener and The Wall Deepener. I would do the wall one first and then do the pleasure one so you can 'test' for a hypnotic response. Sometimes people show no signs of experiencing pleasure. Don't worry they are: some people are just naturally more demonstrative than others.

Exduction: waking them up.

After whacking someone into deep hypnosis you *must* wake them up properly. You can't leave people in fugue states. However everyone wakes up, you can't stay in hypnosis. When starting a session you can give yourself a failsafe: say,

'In a moment you can experience a deep hypnotic trance, if for any reason or emergency you need to awaken then you can do so with all your waking resources instantly available, totally wide awake...but for now, sit back, relax and...etc.'

The golden rule of waking people up is: the longer in trance, the longer it takes to come out. Don't clap your hands like a cheap magician as they awaken or you may very well startle them. I have done it: people look at you like they're thinking −'What did you do that for idiot!' Awaken them gently, kindly as you would a child. Some people will say,

'But it's so nice. I don't want to wake up yet...'
So you say while smiling,
'We're finished now, time to go etc.'
If they still stay under simply say, in a firm clear voice,
'Wakey, wakey rise and shine!'

It always works for me. It's the sort of thing mums/moms say to their children. Set up a post hypnotic command before waking them so that the next time its quicker and easier to get them to go under. More about post hypnotics in another book. Just say...

Post hypnotics.

'If you ever want me to help you/hypnotise you in the future all I will have to say is DEEP SLEEP/CONDITION X (whatever trigger word you want) only within the context of a hypnosis session obviously (reassures they won't become yours or someone else's hypno-gimp!) and you can and will be able to renter a state of trance and hypnosis 50/100 (as preferred by you, who knows what 50 or 100 times 'deeper' means anyway,) times deeper than the one you have experienced easily and quickly.'

You voice tone and speed should be changing at this stage. Speed up a bit and sound less relaxing, more as though you are just about to wake someone up, not quite yet but soon. There should be what I can only describe as a tone of approaching conclusion or finality.

Awakening process.

'I am now going to count from 1-5 and on the count of 5 you will feel fully wide awake and alert, feeling calm, confident and relaxed. Feeling very good.

On 1, gradually awakening, after this session you will feel an inner warm glow of confidence, a renewed optimism for life!

2, Realising how much better you feel, all past tension gone and all unnecessary relaxation leaving your body...feeling more energised!

3, Lighter and brighter, and when you **wake up in a few moments** you'll feel very, very healthy, happier and more centred than before! You'll be lively and feel fine, alert, full of energy and vitality!

4, Normal feelings now returning to each and every muscle group, more aware of your body and the room around you. Feeling so good!

5, Everything back to normal, normal waking breathing, mind clear and very alert! Feeling great and reenergised! And as soon as you are ready open your eyes, wide awake and alert on...5!!!'

If we were doing therapy we'd do more stuff than just the above. But we haven't delivered any therapeutic suggestions really. Again this will be covered in a future book on doing hypnotherapy. So that's it. You've learned all

the basics. You just need some victims, I mean volunteers to practise on. Make sure you get book two on precision hypnotic language: it will take your hypnotic mastery to the next level. One last thing! *For about 4-5 minutes after waking from trance people can be a bit groggy and are still suggestible.* So when they awaken and reorient to the room they're in you can ask, *'Feel good?'*
If they say I feel a bit spacey or anything of that kind just smile and say confidently,
'Yeah, that'll pass in a few seconds.'
But remember they still are suggestible so you can say things like,
'Feel good after that?'
'Was that a nice/interesting experience?'

Some want to discuss what happened and some don't. Make sure they leave a happy bunny. If you want them to experience a degree of amnesia after the session just say during the wake up part,
'You can forget to remember what you can remember to forget,' that will do the trick nicely!

Happy hypnotising!

The following appendices include scripts for you to practise with. I suggest you use 1 on its own. 2-6 can be used as an entire practise session.

Try reading it out on your own before asking for volunteers, it will make you feel more confident. Practice tonality, hypno-voice, waking up voice, downward inflexion on embeds. Bathe your volunteer with the qualities of your voice – if you say *'feel confident'* match the emotion to the state you want them to experience. Most importantly relax, be confident and enjoy yourself. You are ready!

Remember the purpose of this: to practise hypnotising someone, to allow them to experience a trance state and to allow them to feel good – then wake 'em up. Job done.
You could say to a potential volunteer,
'I am learning about hypnosis, would you like me to hypnotise you so you can feel really good? I know exactly what to do.'
Say it with conviction: after all it's true. Who can refuse!

Appendix 1: Betty Erickson Induction.

Notice four things you can see in the room...
four objects...
maybe the way the light hits an object...
Now notice three things you can see...
Now two...
Now one...
That's right...
Just gently...
close your eyes...
Notice four sounds in the environment...
maybe that airplane, the ticking clock...
a certain quality of my voice if you prefer...
Now three sounds...
Now two...
Now one...
Now notice four feelings or sensations...
could be the feel of your palm touching your
jeans perhaps...
the sofa beneath you...
the feel of the shirt on your neck...
Good.
Now three things you feel...
Now two...
Now one...
That's right.
Now, can you **imagine** four pleasant objects
that you've seen...?
could be a cat...
a dog...

a cup...anything...
And when you've done that
imagine three things you've seen...
And two when you're ready...
And one.
Ok...Very good...
now recall four pleasant sounds with your
mind's ear...
a steam train chugging by...
children laughing
a piano playing...
anything you like...
When you've done that
recall more sounds...
Two sounds...
And then just one...
one sound only...
Good, now
can you remember four pleasant sensations?
four textures...
maybe a cat's fur...
the taste of ice cream...
the feel of the breeze against your skin...
whatever you'd like to imagine feeling...
that's right...
Now, when you're ready...
three things you've felt...
And then two when you're ready...
And one...
that's right.
Perfect.

You're doing fantastically.
I am now going to count from 1-3
and on 3 you'll be fully wide awake,
back to full waking consciousness feeling
fantastic!
Ok and 1, more aware of your body
and the room around you!
2, All unnecessary relaxation leaving the body...
feeling wide awake and totally reenergised!
And you can open eyes feeling great! On 3!

Appendix 2: The Rogue Hypnotist's Basic Induction.

In a moment you can experience a deep hypnotic trance, if for any reason or emergency you need to awaken then you can do so with all your waking resources instantly available, totally wide awake...but for now, sit back, relax, get comfy and...

Ok just close your eyes...

It is now time to **feel growing comfort**...'

You don't have to do anything else, just simply pay attention to your breathing...

And now, as you do, take a deep breath and hold it for a moment, that's right, and just **let go** as you slowly release that breath and **relax**...

And again – deep breath in and slowly release that breath and just **relax a bit more**...

When you relax on an out breath – **your comfort only increases**...that's right...

You don't have to do anything at all...nowhere to go...nothing to do as you **go into trance**...Noticing any pleasant sensations, processes, experiences as you **go inside**, now...

Because all you need to do as you just allow certain things to happen...to turn your attention inward and become aware of certain things occurring in your body...in response to these words...

And recognise and experience any reactions within that body to these words...and be able to feel how good they feel as you **feel, really feel a kind of comfort**...

Imagine breathing through your solar plexus... Now, imagine a colour that makes you **feel very calm and comfortable, now...**

Allow a wave of that colour of comfort to begin to spread from the top of your head, all the way down, to the tips of your toes...

All of your muscles becoming softer, letting go now...as you notice any sounds you hear, any words that I say, anything and everything allows your good feelings to only increase, allows you to **drift off**...

You are free to wander and wonder...

As you **relax even more deeply** you can know that the mind and body are one interconnected unit and where the mind leads, the body follows and where the body leads the mind follows...

You may hear the sound of my voice going with you...

Only pleasant thoughts, pleasant images, perhaps one particularly relaxing memory can drift through your mind as you fully **enter this state**.

You don't have to open your eyes or talk, let me do the talking for a while...

Do you *really* think you are awake? (Option but be brave!)

You don't have to understand consciously, your beliefs, your unconscious beliefs are all that matters.

Which part is most comfortable?

Funny to find **all feels well**...

On occasion it can be very good and pleasant enjoying letting go of certain directions and controls to permit unconscious autonomous/independent processes to take over...

You may be wondering what will shift and change first...

And you can easily use all your powers of imagination, intelligence and inner focus ensuring you will achieve all you desire from this session without knowing how you did it consciously...

How much further into trance and hypnosis can you really go?

Enjoy feeling more and more comfortable as you go deeper inside...

You could notice words and notice noticing words...

And the deeper you go, the more wonderful you feel and the more wonderful you feel the deeper you can go, now... that's right!'

As we continue you can **hear my voice** and at other times it might seem quiet or distant and at other times it doesn't matter if you can hear it at all because you can allow a deeper part of you to hear all you need to hear, here/hear and now...

You know that you are the one who is in control as we make even more amazing changes.

And you can process that while I'm quiet...

And anyone can **feel confident** each day...

And you can follow your own associative processes to these words, can you not? Like the word 'comfort' and follow where it leads you...now...

You're eyelid muscles can feel so relaxed that your **'eyes'** easily remain **'closed'** and as they do you feel even more absorbed in pleasant processes...

Each out breath helps melt past tension which floats away into the distance like storm clouds melting, fading away in the sunshine guaranteeing your success...knowing you don't have to do those things you once did...

As a person's mind develops other awareness's, **the body can...rest...**

...You don't have to move unless that movement brings you more of that which you wish...

Appendix 3: The Magic Wall deepener.

See a wall in your mind's eye...
in a moment, not yet but soon,
you'll see numbers going downward from 20-1.
they will appear on that wall.
they'll be a certain helpful colour.
as I count down from 20-1
those numbers will change,
to match the numbers
I am counting **downward now**,
all the way down,
and as they head towards 1
they'll shrink
increasingly so,
like those things in Alice in Wonderland
that changed size.
And before they reach 15
they'll have shrunk so small
that they will have disappeared,
vanished;
just like that.
And when that happens
you will already have entered
a profoundly wonderful state
of deep trance and deep hypnosis
deep hypnotic **SLEEP!**
Deeper than ever before, now...
Ok, here we go...
20, 19, numbers shrinking...
going down...

18, deeper, smaller...
17, even more so...
16, almost there,
going all the way down...
15! Gone completely!
Vanished!
It's so nice, so pleasing...
is it not?

Appendix 4: The Pleasure deepener.

Not yet but soon I will count from 1 to 3 and
say the word BLISS!
When I do you can allow yourself to
**feel absolutely wonderful for no particular
reason**.
feeling good...feeling happy...
feeling content, comfortable...
even **blissful, now**,
better than you have felt for some time.
And when I say DEEPER
you can go 20 times deeper than you were...
and you can feel even better
because the golden rule of hypnosis is,
the deeper you go the better you feel
and the better you feel the deeper
you can go, nooow...
Is that ok with you?
Are you ready?
(Don't wait for a response)
Here we go...
1-2-3 BLISS! (Say it blissfully.)
And that just feels really good doesn't it?
Feeling really good...
DEEPER!
The deeper you go the better you feel
and the better you feel
the deeper you can go...that's right.
And that feels even better doesn't it?
Ok...and again... ('Ok' gets the subconscious

ready.)
1-2-3 BLI-ISS!!
And that feels even better doesn't it?
feeling really good,
even better than before!
DEEPER!
The deeper you go the better you feel
and the better you feel the deeper you can go!
And that does feel even better doesn't it!
Just enjoy these good feelings...
That's right...
And one more time for luck...
1-2-3 BLISS!!!
And that feels really good doesn't it?
Whatever that feeling is you're feeling...
perhaps the best feeling so far?
Learning what you need to learn from this
experience...
because your subconscious is the seat
of your emotions...
it can let you **feel more comfort,**
more confidence, more relaxed alertness
when needed,
bursts of good feelings for no reason..
Even better ones,
more and more and more...
and you can, can you not?
DEEPER!
The deeper you go the better you feel...
And the better you feel the deeper you can go...
Nooooowww!

Deeper and deeper into trance and hypnosis!
Deeper than you've ever been before, now.

Install post hypnotic command.
If you ever want me to help you/hypnotise you
in the future all I will have to say is DEEP
SLEEP/CONDITION X! Only within the context
of a hypnosis session obviously and you can
and will be able to renter a state of trance and
hypnosis 50/100 times deeper than the one you
have experienced easily and quickly. (Delivery
slightly more energised.)

Appendix 5: Awakening process.

I am now going to count from 1-5 and on the count of 5 you will feel fully wide awake and alert, feeling calm, confident and relaxed. Feeling very good.

On 1, gradually awakening, after this session you will feel an inner warm glow of confidence, a renewed optimism for life!

2, Realising how much better you feel, all past tension gone and all unnecessary relaxation leaving your body...feeling more energised!

3, Lighter and brighter, and when **you wake up in a few moments** you'll feel very, very healthy, happier and more centred than before! You'll be lively and feel fine, alert full of energy and vitality!

4, Normal feelings now returning to each and every muscle group, more aware of your body and the room around you. You can forget to remember what you can remember to forget! Feeling so good!

5, Everything back to normal, normal waking breathing, mind clear and very alert! Feeling great and reenergised! And as soon as you are ready open your eyes, wide awake and alert on...5!!!

Feel good?

See you soon for book 2: 'Mastering hypnotic language.' This book series becomes more advanced yet remains easy to learn as it progresses.

You have done well young Padawan Apprentice!

The Rogue Hypnotist signing off. For now…

46352073R00064

Made in the USA
San Bernardino, CA
04 March 2017